HE SENT HIS WORD *and* HEALED ME

HELEN H. WILKS

Order this book online at www.trafford.com
or email orders@trafford.com

Most Trafford titles are also available at major online book retailers.

Print information available on the last page.

ISBN: 978-1-4907-9951-3 (sc)
ISBN: 978-1-4907-9952-0 (e)

Library of Congress Control Number: 2020901119

Scripture taken from The Holy Bible, King James Version. Public Domain

Trafford rev. 02/21/2020

www.trafford.com
North America & international
toll-free: 1 888 232 4444 (USA & Canada)
fax: 812 355 4082

The still small voice…

Is God's way of giving us important valuable information that will become a blessing to us.

All honor and praise goes to God for allowing me to be a recipient of His miraculous deliverance and healing powers. For the opportunity to share my experience and victories with others.

To my wonderful parents. The late Allen and Fannie Hayes; What a blessing it was to have you as my parents. You taught me good. I feel you know how the seeds that you planted in my life has grown. I've never forgotten your teaching me the power of prayer and to always stay prayed up.

To my family extraordinaire; My daughters Traci and Kim. Their husbands Darius and Thomas. Thank you for all you do and continue to do to make my life easier.

To my precious grandchildren; Xavier, Darian, Antonie, Jiarus and William (Lil D). Thank you for bringing so much joy and laughter into my life. Love you to the moon and back. To my special grands that doesn't belong to me; Azari Joi and Doryana, you make me happy. To my niece Bishop Bobbie Williams, thank you for always being there for me through this journey of life, for being my partner in prayer. Look what God has done. And still we stand.

Make new friends and keep the old; one is silver and the other gold. To my gold friends: Janet, Angel and Mrs. Heddie Saulter. When I count my blessings I count you twice. Silver friends-Laura and Ruth H., thank you.

To those who helped cultivate the seed planted in my life: The late Pastor Ray McCluney, Mother Susie McCluney, Pastor Roy Fitzgerald and First Lady Marian Fitzgerald, Pastor Anthony and First Lady Yolanda Stephenson, Elder Beatrice Cannon, My Pastor and Bishop Bobbie Williams, my physicians who along with me believed in the voice, Dr. Sanders, Dr. Smith and Dr. Aquiar. God's blessings be upon you all.

To my readers:

I pray that after reading this book your faith and trust in God's word will be restored. That prayer and speaking God's word along with having faith will allow healing and supernatural manifestation of God's work to take place in your life. Scriptures were taken from the Holy Bible (KJV). Definitions are from the Merriam-Webster dictionary 1974 edition.

THE STILL SMALL VOICE

My first affliction began December 2, 2016. I use the term light affliction because the word of God says our "light affliction," which is but for a moment, worketh for us a far more exceeding and eternal weight of glory; (II Corinthians 4:17). I know that after reading my story you will probably think there's nothing light about her life experiences.

On December 2, 2016 I went to my primary physician because I was feeling tired and had shortness of breath. I was examined and given an E.K.G. I was told nothing was wrong except my E.K.G. reading was a little different than the last time; but attributed it to growing older. I told him no thanks, that's not it, I know my body. I know when all's not well. He then said I probably had over eaten at Thanksgiving and was having severe indigestion. I was given a prescription for indigestion and told to take magnesium to help restore my energy. I knew that wasn't the case and I wasn't accepting that explanation.

My insurance didn't cover emergency room visits unless their office was closed.

My plan was to visit Urgent Care Sunday after church and have them check me out. Saturday night as I was preparing for bed it became hard for me to breathe. Pain began to start at my left temple and continue down my left side down to my feet. In a couple of minutes I felt a part of me began to feel numb. I called my daughter to let her know I needed to go to Urgent Care. While I waited for her to arrive, I began to talk to God. When we feel like we can't pray, we can talk to Him like the friend we know He is. I began to tell Him this was the worst pain I've had in my life, even worst than childbirth. I said, "Lord I'm beginning to get a little uneasy about this thing, I need You to talk to me and let me know what's going on in this body of mine. He answered and said, "there's a blood clot in your left leg." I began to thank Him and give Him praise, for I know my Savior's voice.

When I arrived at Urgent Care and told them my symptoms, they didn't believe me, especially about a blood clot in my left leg. They said it was my heart and they began to do heart related stuff, E.K.G. and put me on oxygen. I kept saying there's a blood clot in my left leg. But they were determined to do their doctor thing on what they thought was wrong. Finally they reached the conclusion that nothing was wrong and they would give me pain medicine for the pain and check back on Monday with my regular physician if I was still in pain. I asked them again to check my left leg and if they didn't I would go some place else. They wanted to know why I kept saying that: We checked you out and according to your symptoms, nothing was found. My response to them was that "this voice told me there's a blood clot in my leg. Needless to say they gave each other a this is a nut case look. One of them asked, "you said this voice told you that there's a clot in your leg?" I looked from one to the other and said yes, that's exactly what I said. I said since I'm paying; why not do what I ask? If there's nothing there I'll do what I think is the best for me next. They said okay, if you insist. Before they could put my whole body into the machine they were pulling me out and telling someone to call their emergency transportation.

When the E.M.T. workers arrived the nurse said "we were about to send her home but she kept telling us this voice said there's a blood clot in her left leg." The male attendant said "so this voice told you there's a clot in your leg, huh?" I answered yes with a bit of an attitude; by now I was beginning to think they are messing with my Jesus and I wasn't going along with that. My grandkids reminds me that He's our Jesus too, Nana. When we got out to the ambulance the male attendant told the lady "I'm going to break the rules and let you drive. I want to sit in the back with Ms. Wilks. As we began pull away from the building he said, "Ms. Wilks you do know what that voice was don't you?" I answered yes, It's God speaking to me through the Holy Spirit. He smiled and said "I'm a Christian and I didn't want to miss out on the opportunity of not knowing that the voice you heard was that of the Holy Spirit." I told him I knew but when I said it to the Urgent care workers the way they looked, if I had said Jesus spoke to me I might have ended up elsewhere. He and I talked and witnessed to each other from High Point to Greensboro. We talked about the goodness of God and all that He has done for our family as well as ourselves. When we arrived at Moses Cone he told them he was delivering someone special and to make sure I was treated as such, and that he would be back to check on me. Thank God for sending His servant to minister to me at that moment in my life.

> And all things, whatsoever ye shall ask in prayer, believing, ye shall receive. (Matthew 21:22)

Notes:

WAKE UP CALL

U pon arriving at Moses Cone Hospital I was placed in intensive care. I remained there for three days. I was hooked up to several machines and was given oxygen to help with my breathing. When I looked around and saw I.C.U. on my door I thought their rooms must be full and they placed me in here. Little did I know then, it was the place I needed to be. I want you to know that God will give you peace in the midst of the worst storms.

I did not know that the left side of my body was completely shut down. Because of the blood clot, blood was unable to flow through that side as it should. The left chamber of my heart was not able to function properly. Thanks be to God the right side began to do the work for both sides, which caused my heart to become enlarged. My being alive was a miracle in itself.

The doctor came in and asked, how I was feeling? I answered him like I always respond to others, "I'm good, hope you are." His reply was no you're not, you're sick and its not looking good for you right now. Before he came in a nurse and I was talking and we were going to pray. She was a believer and I knew the power of prayer. Now back to Mr. Doctor. I asked him about removing the oxygen from my nose because it kept falling out. He said he couldn't and that I would probably be on oxygen for the rest of m life. He said I had some type of heart problem that was a threat to my life. He named some letters for the condition he was talking about. I didn't go into details with him about it but said to myself the devil is a liar. I asked him if he believed in prayer. He said he did. I informed him that the nurse and I was getting ready to pray; that where two or more are gathered together in His name, He's in the midst of them (Matthew 18:20). We were two and adding a third would be even better. That was not happening! He said "no, you need to be thinking about getting better so that you can have the surgery you need." That didn't go well with me, I took that as an insult to my Jesus. I kindly asked him, I think, to get out of my room with all of his negativity and he probably didn't know how to pray anyway. After his departure the nurse and I laughed uncontrollably. I thought I wouldn't have to see him again and breathed a sigh of relief. Wrong, as you will learn later.

And the prayer of faith shall save the sick, and the Lord shall raise him up; and if he have committed sins, they shall be forgiven him. (James 5:15)

Beloved, I wish above all things that thou mayest prosper and be in health, even as thy soul prospereth. (3 John 1:2)

Notes:

LIFE CHANGING
MOMENTS

U pon leaving I.C.U. my next stop was C.C.U. (Critical
Care Unit). Again I am thinking, are there no vacancies in
regular rooms? I still had my peace in the midst of life's storm.
In critical care I was introduced to my surgeon, cardiologist
and my primary care physician. Yep you guessed it, the doctor
I asked to leave my room. He didn't come alone he brought
the cardiologist with him. I'm thinking for backup. He spoke
what he had to say and retreated as if to say not today lady.
The cardiologist explained things about my heart to me and
asked if I had any questions. I asked did he think it was wise
to have surgery. He promised me that he would not allow them
to operate until he thought I was able to go through it. There
was something about him that gave me comfort. I felt this isn't

a man about the heart, this is a man that has a heart and truly cares about his patients. He told me he would be there with me during my surgery.

I'd had so many tests, hooked up to so many machines, blood drawn every two or three hours to see if the medication I was given was dissolving the clots. I had a clot in my left leg, four in my lungs and one that had landed behind my heart. They thought maybe I had a hole in my heart. I kept saying Lord I know you're going to take me through this. If not Your will for me will be done. I still had that peace that even I couldn't understand. God is awesome! He has a way of letting you know He's in control and He's got you. I will explain that phrase later.

The surgeon comes in with several other doctors. He explained to them that he had never seen a case like mine in his life. He said her left side is completely shut down and one side of her heart is carrying her whole body. As the clots are breaking up some are going up to her heart and her heart is knocking them back out. It's as if God is saying "you can't have her, her heart belongs to me, she's mine." He said I don't understand this, this beats anything I've ever seen. Little did he know he had just prophesied over my life. I had just witnessed God's Holy Spirit again speaking through someone else. God can and will do anything He chooses to do to let His will be known in your life. I wanted to tell the doctors don't worry everything's going to be alright, God got me. I prayed for every patient at Moses Cone, for their healing and deliverance of anything they needed to be rid of. I prayed for God to anoint and guide my surgeon's hands. I tried to focus on others and not myself because I felt a surety of what God was going to do for me. Someone thought a hole was in my heart because a clot had landed behind my heart. They didn't understand how it got there unless it passed through a hole. I let the doctors have their moment because God and I already had ours and it was settled. My faith gave me the peace I needed. No hole was found.

For God has granted me life and favour, and thy visitation hath preserved my spirit. (Job 10:12)

Now faith is the substance (assurance) of things hoped for, the evidence of things not seen. (Hebrews 11:1)

My flesh and my heart faileth: but God is the strength of my heart, and my portion for ever. (Psalm 73:26)

substance - the quality of being important; valid. something that proves ground for belief. significant; main part of a lesson.

evidence - body of facts; information indicating faith, dependence or trust in someone or something. confident, or trustful, truth, something you see or experience.

Notes:

SURGERY

GOTTA PUT THE WORD ON IT

After receiving blood thinner medication to dissolve the clots, the one in my leg would not dissolve. I was told I had a total of six in all. Four in my lungs, one in my left leg. It required four hours of surgery for removal. As I was being rolled down the hallway to surgery something a former pastor said came to mind. He was being taken to surgery for what the doctors said was cancer. As he was being taken to the operating room, he began to pray for every patient in the room he passed. Once he reached his destination and the doctor did one last check to see where to begin to remove the cancer, there was none there. He was completely healed. God wants us to focus and care for others more than for ourselves. When we decrease, He increases. I followed in his footsteps and did the same thing. I wasn't rid of the clot but I had a peace that surpasseth my understanding.

The nurse that was prepping me for surgery said, "do you do anything other than smile?" I had no idea I had a smile on my face. Smiling doesn't come easy in situations such as mine. Thanks be to God everything went well, or so we thought. When my drainage container was checked, I was losing too much blood. Within two hours I was taken back to O.R. I think maybe my smile had disappeared and I was thinking, what now Lord? An Elder told me in times of trouble she recites the twenty-third Psalm. As they were rolling me down the same route I started saying the twenty-third Psalm. As I got to yea though I walk through the valley I stopped; not me. I refuse to allow the word death to enter my thoughts or come out of my mouth. Thank God for knowing His word. My mind went immediately to the woman with the issue of blood. I cried out to God with everything within me. I said God I'm kind of like the woman with the issue of blood. I cannot touch the hem of Your garment, but I am asking the name of Jesus to stop the bleeding.

When I awoke from the surgery I was so disoriented I though I was in the morgue. Too much putting me to sleep medication I think. I looked to my right and several silver empty cots were there. They had no cover on them and I'm thinking this is not good at all. Do they think I'm dead? I was afraid to look to the left because I feared dead bodies would be on that side. I don't want to knowingly share space with the dead. I guess my spirit of fear had left me for a moment. I thought, I'll just lie here quietly and not look left or right, now's the time to look up more than ever. When someone comes I'll let them know I'm alive. Now I can say that was spiritual humor. When the nurse came to check my vitals I asked, why did you put me here? She could tell by the tone of my voice I wasn't a happy recoverer. I guess she was wondering what happen to the smile. She said, "OK Ms. Wilks I'll take you to your room right now." I never did look to the left, I felt that it was best for me not to. Later the surgeon came in and said, "Ms. Wilks, I'm so sorry I went back into your leg again, when I got in there it was as dry as a bone, there was no sign of bleeding. I panicked because I knew you couldn't continue to lose blood at that rate." My God, my Awesome Magnificent God had done it again.

> And it shall come to pass, that before they call, I will answer; and while they are yet speaking, I will hear. (Isaiah 65:24)

> For she said, If I may touch but his clothes, I shall be whole. (Mark 5:28)

> And he looked round about to see her that had done this thing. (Mark 5:32)

> And he said unto her, Daughter, thy faith hath made thee whole; go in peace, and be whole of thy plague. (Mark 5:34)

> Someone should be praising God now! Thinking of His many blessings, His healings and power of deliverance.

Notes:

IT'S NOT FOR OUR UNDERSTANDING

My daughters Traci and Kim had been by my side since the visit to Urgent Care. Traci is the one that steps up and takes charge. She was going back and forth with the doctors and nurses about what was being done and why. If she wasn't there when changes were being made, she wanted to be notified about the changes that was being made and why. She was so into everything that was going on, they asked me who was the mother. By her working in the medical field she wanted to be abreast of everything that was happening. She's outspoken whereas Kim is the quiet one. She watches and prays. I call her my prayer warrior and intercessor.

I guess the smile had returned to my face because Traci had taken all she could take. She said "Momma. I'm tired of you scaring us to death and you lying there acting like nothing's happening. "Did you know you almost died? You need to get serious about what's going on." I guess the burden was getting a little too heavy for her to bear. Even though I didn't feel sick, everyone was saying I was critically ill. I thought I'd better toss in some more sickness scriptures to make sure all bases were covered. I asked Kim is she was okay after Traci had expressed her feelings. She nodded yes. A nurse asked, "is your daughter Kim alright, she just sits with her head down and doesn't say anything." I told her she's okay, she's just praying for her mother. I have a close knit family, we're always there for each other. I have two daughters, five grandchildren and two son-in-laws. Small but large in kindness and love.

Now back to the good stuff. According to the doctors and medical staff I was suppose to be in severe pain and discomfort. Which would require medication for pain every four hours. I had no pain which baffled the entire medical staff. They suggested I take something anyway before the pain began to get bad. I told them I was not in pain and didn't need the medication. They said there was no way that I could not be in pain. That it was impossible to not have pain. I told them when I was in pain and needed medication I would let them know. I never told anyone that I was a christian. My father always said to let the life you live speak for you. A nurse came into the room and said, "Ms Wilks, I'm a christian too and God would want us to take medicine when we are in pain." Now this was beginning to be too much. I kindly replied, "thank you, I have sense enough to take medicine when I'm in pain." I thought it was over but they kept trying to give me pain medicine I didn't need. I was labeled the stubborn patient who didn't listen. When the shifts were changing they would stand outside my door and talk about how I refused to take medicine and other things I did when I pushed the call button and waited twenty minutes and they didn't show. When you are standing outside someone's door talking about them even though its midnight you might need to check to make sure they are asleep. Then again, maybe they wanted me to hear. Nevertheless what the devil meant for bad, God meant it for my good.

Now I've been moved from Critical Care to Recovery and release. The oxygen was removed and I was breathing on my own. A therapist came to take me for short walks, monitor my heartbeat and breathing. Didn't make it twenty five steps before my heart rate went up too high. The next day I was able to walk from one end of the hall to the other and I was steady running off at the mouth. I was doing so good he said, "let me know when you get tired and we'll go back to your room." He must have gotten tired of me and my mouth and was ready to put an end to it. Next day a little more monitoring and therapy and I was told I'll probably be going home in a day to two. My primary care physician, the one I asked to leave my room came in and said, "I heard you wanted to go home, first you need to be truthful about the pain you're in. You shouldn't say stuff just because you want to go home." I sat up in the bed and was getting ready to say the wrong thing to him. Something (the voice) said, "don't answer, he doesn't understand." I laid back down and thought, where is my Traci when I need her? If she was there and took his words as saying you're lying and you need to stop; when she got finish with him I would have gotten an early release ready or not. Lol. That's a joke on Traci, she wouldn't have, I hope.

Later that evening I was told that he was working on my release papers and I would be going home the next day. Two nurses came in around nine that night and asked me would I at least take a Tylenol so that I would get a good night's rest. I needed that since I would be leaving the next day. I needed the sleep since I hadn't been sleeping well. I though to be left alone I'll do it. Let them have the privilege of saying we got her to take a Tylenol. When she brought the pill in I said, "this doesn't look like a Tylenol, it doesn't have the lettering on it." She said, "its a hospital Tylenol." I flipped the pill several times before I decided to take it. About two o'clock in the morning I woke up to three nurses in my room observing. I asked if there was a problem. They said that they were just observing me. Something had showed up on the machine and they came to check it out. I said, "that wasn't Tylenol you gave me was it?' I'm still waiting for the answer. I'm thinking they finally got some pain medicine in me but they paid the cost. They looked very uncomfortable. I was released from the hospital later that afternoon.

A physical and occupational therapist was assigned to me for twice a week visitation. So I would be receiving four days of therapy a week to aid in my recovery. They were not allowed to come out until I had a prescription filled for some pain medication that I needed to take after the visit or before the visit. A week later my insurance company called and insisted on me filling the prescription so my therapy could start. I got it filled because I knew I needed therapy to complete my healing process. After two weeks they wanted to use my space to do whatever and not to continue working with me. They had shown me what to do so I told them I no longer needed their services. I told them my insurance was to be billed for only the days that they showed up not the six weeks. They apologized, I accepted and wished them well. I did my own therapy and exercises. The doctors were taken aback on how quickly I was recovering, even the scars on my leg became almost invisible. What they had predicted to happen in a year was happening in four to six months.

> For which cause we faint not; but though our outward man perish, yet the inward man is renewed day by day. For our light affliction, which is but for a moment, worketh for us a far more exceeding and eternal weight of glory; (2 Corinthians 4:16, 17)

I had fainted, unless I had believed to see the goodness of the LORD in the land of the living. (Psalm 27:13)

That it might be fulfilled which was spoken by Esaias the prophet, saying, Himself took our infirmities, and bare our sicknesses. (Matthew 8:17)

Notes:

VI

ALL THINGS WORKING
FOR MY GOOD

As of now I am scheduled for a yearly checkup with my primary physician and my cardiologist. And every six months with my hematologist. I speak complete healing of my body because I know God's word destroys the enemy's work, so will believing God's word over man. My heart has returned to its normal size and is working as God created it to work.

After overcoming this light affliction in my life, friends and family say there was nothing light about what I went through. I began to do a replay of my life. When I thought about all I've been through, I realized how blessed I've been and that God's favor has continuously been upon me. I had favor with God and man. When I was given lemons, I found a way to sweeten them so they became lemonade. When I was broken

I proclaimed that the potter will put me back together again; stronger and wiser. I want to share some of these things with you too. So you'll know God is always with us even when we don't realize it. He's there working it out for our good. As the saying goes, "if He brings us to it, He'll take us through it."

One of the things that comes to mind when I realized that the Holy Spirit spoke to me was when I was working at a job where sometimes I needed to work on Sundays. I finally told the manager that I as well as my daughters were involved in several church activities and wanted to attend church more regularly. I finally decided to leave and look for a new job. I was at work one day and I said, "Lord I'm getting tired of this, when are You going to get me out of this place?" I heard a voice say "August." I looked around to see if anyone looked as if they had heard what I just did. Everyone was looking and acting normal. I said, "OK Lord, August it is." I was happy and thanking God in my mind. I didn't know where or how, all I knew was that I would be leaving there in August.

I can't remember how I heard that the school system was hiring. I went there and applied for a job as a teacher assistant. I was told they had several hundred applicants for that one job. Certified teachers were applying as well as others with college degrees. I was called in for an interview. I was told it was their custom to interview everyone they thought would qualify for the job. When I went in for the interview I was prayed up. I had prayed to God give me the right words to say. I was suppose to hear something from them in two weeks. I waited patiently for that call to come. When it didn't come by the middle of the third week I decided to call him and ask had the position been filled. I called and identified myself and told him I was checking on the position I had applied for. Thanks be to God I did. He told me he had called and left a message with my husband to call him if I still wanted the job. Since he hadn't heard back from me, he was getting ready to call and offer it to someone else. He said the job was mine if I wanted it. I did and I accepted. That was around the first week in August and within three weeks I would be starting my new job. I am humming what God has for me is for me. I know without a doubt that He will work it out. What God has for me, it is for me. I gave notice to my employer that I would be leaving. He said, "that's nice, you were lucky." No not lucky, blessed. My new job came with benefits, paid sick leave, insurance, holidays, retirement fund, and summers off to enjoy time with my daughters. I stayed with them for sixteen years.

> Delight thyself also in the LORD; and he shall give thee the desires of thine heart. 5 Commit thy way unto the LORD; trust also in him; and he shall bring it to pass. (Psalm 37:4, 5)

Notes:

BELIEVE

A couple of years into working with the school system my husband and I separated. I was left with the responsibility of raising my two young daughters. I started working a part-time job to supplement my income. I was told by some christians the more crosses you bear the more stars in your crown. I felt that I had so many stars in my crown and it was getting so heavy I could hardly hold my head up to see where I was going. I had to let go so I could hold my head up to see where I was going. His mindset was, as a christian whatever was done to me regardless of how it affected our children, it was suppose to be forgiven. Sometimes prayer doesn't change things at the time they need to be changed. Our time is not God's time. Soliciting the help of our daughters we prayed, prayed, and prayed some more. One night I looked up and they were standing in my bedroom door with this strange look on their face. I asked, "what was wrong?" They said, "we decided that we are not going to pray for daddy anymore. The more we pray the worse he gets." It caught me by surprise. I didn't really know how to answer them. I said, "Okay, if that's how you feel." At the moment I didn't think to tell them that in spite of what seem to be happening he still needed our prayers. He was dealing with demons that only God could deliver him from. I continued to pray for him to surrender his life to God. To be the man God intended him to be. To be a good father and role model for his daughters. To be a good husband for some woman. Not for me, as the saying goes; I was done.

I was not able to receive the assistance that I need in order to help him. I was not blameless. I accepted my part in the failure of our marriage. I knew I had my responsibility as a wife and a mother, and he had his as a father and husband. A husband is suppose to be the head of the household and lead by example. I apologized and asked if we could co-parent our daughters. I wanted him to be a part of their lives. He said, "no." I guess he was done too. Regardless, I had the most important man in my life, you guessed right, my Jesus.

And who is he that will harm you, if ye be followers of that which is good? (I Peter 3:13)

Thy word is a lamp unto my feet, and a light unto my path. (Psalm 119:105)

Notes:

VIII

ALL THINGS WORKING
FOR MY GOOD

I always wanted to have my own daycare. I would plan to leave my job and get iffy about it. I would have a Plan A for it being a success and a Plan B if it failed. Until I made up my mind that with God on my side I didn't need a Plan B. I was wavering in my faith. God wants us to stand strong and not waver in our faith. He will do what He said He would do. I was on my way to work one morning and a minister on the radio was saying how he wanted to be in the ministry full time but felt he wouldn't be able to support his family. He said he prayed about it and decided to trust God. He quit his job that day and told his mom and brother what he had done. They asked, "had he lost his mind? How was he going to support his wife and children without the job?" He said, "here I am today a full time

minister, has lost nothing. I'm even on the radio doing great."
He said he stepped out on faith, believing God's word. That
message stayed with me all day into the late hours of the night.
I decided these words had been spoken for me to hear. I said,
"okay God if you did it for him, You'll do it for me."

It was nearing the Christmas holidays. I decided that when
we got out for Christmas break I was not returning. I wrote up
my resignation and took it over to the Administration Office.
They tried to talk me out of it. I wasn't getting any younger
and knew now was the time to pursue my dream. I didn't look
back only up and ahead. I started ordering the things I needed
for a daycare before I had gotten the space. Once I agreed on
a place I was so busy preparing it I hadn't thought about my
need for children to have a daycare. When it came to me I said,
"I'll make fliers and ask businesses to let me post them in their
store." In the meantime I was praying and telling God what
He said about supplying my need. I knew He knew. I needed
children for my daycare. He knew it even before the revelation
came to me. I had the fliers printed and ready to go. Before I
could place one flier, my daycare was filled with a waiting list.
My youngest daughter was working at a Child Development
Center. She called and told me they were closing their infants
and toddlers rooms down and she was giving the parents my
name and number so they could set up an appointment with
me. I've got to pause and get myself together. My Jesus, my
Savior. God is good. Thank you Jesus. I set up appointments
so that the child and the parent could come together. I was able
to choose the ones I wanted to attend because I had more than
enough. I had a great Open House. I knew for sure God had
helped me in choosing the ones that I needed for my daycare.
My motto was: Building strong minds and self-esteem in young
children.

The LORD will perfect that which concerneth me: thy mercy, O LORD, endureth for ever: forsake not the works of thine own hands. (Psalm 138:8)

For we walk by faith, not by sight: (2 Corinthians 5:7)

Notes:

WALKING BY FAITH

To have a successful daycare you need transportation for field trips and other outings. I began searching for transportation for my precious little ones. I told their parents they were mine as well as theirs while in my care. They all called me Nana, the same as my grandchildren. When I found the van I wanted I had a name it and claim it attitude. What I had claimed didn't fit into my financial budget. The salesman explained to me if I wanted a Streamliner I had to pay the price. I decided to settle for a regular brand new boat. He said, "I have the perfect thing for you, we're cleaning it up now. It will be more affordable." When he said that I thought not me. When I saw the van I thought he's got to be kidding. He said, "come into my office so we can talk." Before he could tell me about the great deal I was getting I told him I didn't want it. I asked him would he want his kids to ride in something like that? I have to think of their safety as well as mine. Plus, God doesn't want me to have any junk.

Little did I know when I was talking the owner of the dealership was standing in the doorway listening. I told the salesman how much I was paying for a down payment and what I wanted the payments to be. I said I was going to other dealerships and see what they had to say about my offer. That was on a Saturday afternoon. Sunday I was at the altar praying for God to intervene on my behalf. When I left that dealership I went back home. As I was at the altar praying little did I know that two other people sitting in a church had me on their mind too. The car salesman and the dealership owner. The salesman told me he decided to go by the dealership after church to see what he could work out for me. While he was there the owner showed up. He told him, that lady that was in here talking to you yesterday has been on my mind. I came to see what I can do to help her. He said, "there's something about her that has stayed with me since I heard her in here talking." The two were talking and agreeing on the same thing.

Another problem I had was I was self-employed. I had no forms for them to check my income. I had just opened my daycare four months prior. They had to accept my word as to what my total monthly income would be. I had told them I was going to use my car plus cash as a down payment. Monday morning around 10:00 AM, I got a call from the salesman. He said, "Ms. Wilks the owner and I worked something out for you. We have a van we think you will like." He asked if I could meet with him within the next hour. I said I would. It took me a little longer than I thought to get someone to help watch the kids. I was running late. He called again to see if I was coming. Blessings were chasing me down and overtaking me. When I arrived I was escorted outside to a brand new 2000 Dodge Caravan. He asked, "is this good enough for you?" The year was 2000, the van was 2000. I thought I was going to break out into a Holy Ghost dance on that car lot. A brand new van financed by the owner of the dealership. I did the paperwork, got my keys and couldn't get the van out of the parking space. My car was a little Ford Escort, so it felt like I was driving a bus. A salesman came up and said let me get this for you and head you off the lot before you tear up our stuff. He got me on my way and I praised God and cried all the way back to the daycare. I felt like I had my Streamliner after all. I ordered a personal tag for my van that said "NHISNAME."

> And beside this, giving all diligence, add to your faith virtue; and to virtue knowledge; (2 Peter 1:5)

> virtue - active power of accomplish, strength, mainly strength and courage. commendable quality, a standard of righteousness.

> knowledge - understanding gained by actual experience. clear perception of truth. something learned and kept in mind.

Notes:

X

YOU CAN'T MAKE
ME DOUBT HIM

I had a sign in my daycare that was written by an anonymous person. In it, it stated that when their life is over that they didn't want to be remembered by the car they drove, the house they lived in, their bank account or the clothes they wore. They wanted to be remembered by the difference they made in the life of a child. They felt that then their living would not have been in vain. My daily goal has been to make a difference in some child or adult's life; with a smile, kind word or deed. My daycare motto was: Building strong minds and self-esteem in young children. Kindness, respect and encouragement comes without cost. If we would take a few minutes each day to realize how blessed we are, then paying it forward will be easy.

Before I go any further let me tell you about me. I don't want you to get the idea that I am a perfect christian. I am far from perfect. None of us are. We all sin and fall short of what God wants us to be. We all sin knowingly and unknowingly. I pray daily for forgiveness of my sins and short comings. My siblings and I were raised up in church. This was required of us by our parents until we were grown and out of our parents house. I remember not feeling well one Sunday and missed church. Later that evening a friend stopped by to ask if I would go walking with her around the neighborhood. Asked my mom would it be okay, she said "no, if you were too sick to go to church this morning you are too sick to go out this afternoon."

My father was a praying man, who read and studied his bible. As a young mother he talked to me about knowing God's word and being prayed up. Ministers from different denominations would come visit him and discuss the bible. He stood firm on his faith and belief. When I began to read my bible, teach Sunday School and Vacation Bible School, things I felt a little unsure about I would ask him. I guess he wanted to know how I was progressing. He would call me and after making sure all was well. He would say turn to a book and chapter of the bible, read it and tell me what you think it mean. Before I could say anything else he would hang up. I would become a nervous wreck. I would start praying to God for knowledge and revelation of His word. I didn't want to tell him the wrong thing. If he and I didn't agree on a verse he would explain to me why he took it to mean a different thing. He would say though we have a different understanding of it, it didn't mean one of us was wrong, just that we had a different interpretation. Never did he say I'm right and you are wrong. He said to ask God for revelation of His word. When I would ask him to pray for me for a certain thing he would say I've already prayed for that. He would say I pray for things and protection for things that hasn't happened. When it does happen I don't worry or fret because I know I've already talked to God about it and its in His hands. I took my dad's advice, (always try to stay prayed up). There's power in prayer and the word of God. I remember older people saying prayer is the key to heaven and faith unlocks the door. He also said to treat others the way you want them to treat you and don't give anyone something you wouldn't want to have or use for yourself.

> But thou, when thou prayest, enter into thy closet, and when thou hast shut thy door, pray to thy Father which is in secret; and thy Father which seeth in secret shall reward thee openly.(Matthew 6:6)

> Now faith is the substance of things hoped for, the evidence of things not seen.(Hebrews 11:1) Please read the eleventh chapter of Hebrews.

> For all have sinned, and come short of the glory of God; (Romans 3:23)

Notes:

HE MADE A WAY

I recall another time when I had to have gall bladder surgery. I had been feeling ill on and off for several months. My doctor gave me a physical and a sonogram and found nothing wrong. I got sick one morning and couldn't keep anything on my stomach. I called the doctor and was told not to come into the office because it was flu season and it sounded like I had the flu. He called in a prescription and told me to drink tea. Again his diagnosis didn't feel right with me. But I went along and prayed along. I was lying in bed one night and my side began to hurt and my stomach began making funny noises. I was thinking and praying Lord what can this be? The voice said, "its your gall bladder." I said, "okay Lord, I'll go to the emergency room after church tomorrow." The next morning I was getting ready for church the voice said, "go to the E.R. now." I told my daughters I had a change of plan. I was going to the E.R. instead of church.

When I arrived I was told my doctor was out of town and would be back on Monday. The doctor on call told them to give me something to ease the pain and to come into the office Monday. The nurse came in and gave me a shot and said she would be back shortly to see if it was working. Nothing happened. She asked my daughters if she gave me another shot and it knocked me out could they get someone to help get me in the house? They said they could. She gave me another shot and said this is going to do it. She left me lying on the table to get someone to take me to the car. When she came back instead of being drowsy I was walking around the room praying. She yelled "no, get on the bed you are going to pass out and burst your head on the floor. You should be sleep by now." I told her I was not sleepy and I was in more pain now than before. She said she couldn't give me anymore medicine because she had given me enough to knock a horse out. I would have to leave and see my doctor tomorrow. Never said a word about admitting me or doing tests to see what was really going on. Maybe that was the way man's system worked but my God doesn't work that way.

A doctor that knew my girls came into the E.R. and saw them sitting there. He asked why were they there. They explained to him what was going on. He told them to come with him and he would see what was happening. He walked in the room and asked, what was wrong? When I looked at him to answer him, He said, "my Lord your eyes has a yellowish look. You have jaundice in your body. Let me admit you and start antibiotics immediately." If one doesn't do it right, God will send another one. My gall bladder was in such awful shape it had begun to poison my system. I had emergency surgery the next morning. The surgeon said it was one of the worst case he had ever seen. He began the surgery, got tired and had to let another surgeon finish up. My friend that was waiting with my girls said, "I was scared, it took them so long. I Thought you had gone to glory." Not so, God's word will destroy the enemy's work. What the devil meant for bad, God meant it for my good.

My recovery took longer than the usual time because of the condition my body was in. It took me eight weeks before I was able to return to work. When I returned to work the principal and several employees told me they were worried about me because I didn't look well. Then there were those who told me about people who had what I had and died. Lol. Their story just let me know that God's favor was upon me. That He loves me and cares for me. Not just me but everyone. I hope my stories, I call them my testimonies isn't being a downer to you. I want everyone to know what God is able to do. He loves and cares for us all, even with our imperfection. When the word says we all sin and fall short of the glory of God, it means no one is perfect. His grace and mercy is given to us all. He loves us not because of but in spite of.

> And God is able to make all grace abound toward you; that ye, always having all sufficiency in all things, may abound to every good work: (2 Corinthians 9:8) (every earthly blessing)

> For by grace are ye saved through faith; and that not of yourselves: it is the gift of God: (Ephesians 2:8)

> grace - help given man by God. help in overcoming temptation and sin, through divine grace, a virtue coming from God.

> It is of the LORD'S mercies that we are not consumed, because his compassions fail not. 23 They are new every morning: great is thy faithfulness. (Lamentations 3:22, 23)

> mercy - compassion shown to an offender. price paid. blessings resulting from divine favor.

Notes:

JESUS LOVES ME

Years later I was told something was showing up in my blood work, they weren't sure what it was. I ran a temperature and was having chills. I guess you are thinking woe is me. Count it all joy, for I am an overcomer. When I had the blood clot issue I began to think of my past life. I knew I had been blessed but had never realized just how blessed my life had been.

I was dubbed the name superwoman by many of my friends. I pursued my dreams, worked several jobs to support my girls. I made sure they did well in school, attended all of their school functions, made sure we spent quality time together, made sure they went to college. Both graduated from college with honors. P.T.A.s were scheduled for fifteen minutes for every class segment. I wanted to be represented in all of their classes. I would spend seven minutes in one and then rush to the other for seven minutes. Their teachers wanted to know why I put myself through that. I did not want them to not be represented at P.T.A. I wanted both of them to be represented by a parent.

Back to the blood issue. I was given medicine to take for couple of days, then return for more blood work. I became so ill when I took the first pill. I didn't take another one. I was lying in bed talking to God, telling Him I can't take the medicine, its making me sicker. I remember the word said we have power and dominion over all earthly things. That we would lay hands on the sick and they would recover. I thought if we can do that for others then it should work for us. I began to pray and lay hands on myself and decree my healing in the name of Jesus and by the authority of His holy word. I proclaimed that by His stripes and the blood of the Lamb we are healed and made whole. I returned to the doctor for my follow up. I was told the medicine had worked and everything was cleared up. You and I know it wasn't the medicine that healed me God showed up and did it again. I would always say Jesus loves me, I'm His favorite child. I would get the yeah, right look but no one would challenge me. I guess they thought I had to be a brick short of a load to say something like that. I wanted them to say He loves me too or He loves everybody.

> He shall not be afraid of evil tidings: his heart
> is fixed, trusting in the LORD. (Psalm 112:7)

> And call upon me in the day of trouble: I will
> deliver thee, and thou shalt glorify me. (Psalm
> 50:15)

Notes:

HE'LL DO WHAT HE
SAID HE'LL DO

My dream car has always been a Mercedes. Nothing made me happier than being out driving and see a lady, retirement age or older driving a Mercedes. To me it said I worked hard and I rewarded myself with this. If they were wearing sunglasses it made my smile even bigger. A few years before retirement I began looking at Mercedes. My mom began to have some health problems. I was trying to continue to work and be her caretaker. This began to be very stressful for me. My doctor said it was putting me at risk health wise. I was told if I kept going at the rate I was going more than likely I would end up having a stroke or heart attack. Since I was a year from early retirement I decided to close daycare down at the end of the school year. I said Lord here I go again totally depending on You. I was standing in the sunroom looking out the window thinking how was I going to work things out financially. I said well God I guess there goes my Mercedes. The voice said, "don't say that." I said well God I guess You know I'll trust You.

A couple of months later my son-in-law told me he had found me a Mercedes. We'll go check it out after church Sunday. He had asked the man who owned the repair shop about it. He was told the car had been sitting there for several months. Someone had taken it there to be checked out and never came back for it. He couldn't believe he had overlooked it since he visited his friend's shop regularly. It wasn't my time. He looked in the car and found the owner's information. When he spoke with him he was told someone wanted to test drive it and have it checked out. They took the car and never came back. He didn't get any information on them so he couldn't file any charges with no information. When discussing the price, he told my son-in-law to find out how much the mechanic charged, plus the storage fee and he would factor that in the price. He gave him a price, and when he said his mother-in-law wanted it, the man reduced the price, and paid for what needed to be done at the D.M.V. I think he had mentioned my name again. I ended up paying cash for the Mercedes. God had made a way the day He spoke to me in the sunroom.

We took it to a mechanic to to get the gas line, oil and other stuff checked out since the car had been sitting for awhile. I was going to put new tires on it. When pay time came, again my son-in-law said, "this is my mother-in-law's car. He charged me half price for my tires and the other stuff was free. By this time my son-in-law was in a tizzy. He said, "if I had known this I would have brought the car for myself." I said, "and you would have paid the full price for the car, tires, checkup, D.M.V. title fee, and inspection fee. Didn't you notice every time you said mother-in-law things changed. That was my blessing God had for me, not you." I don't know if that made him any happier but I was elated. I had my Mercedes.

I named her Grace. Grace means favor. Unearned kindness. To bend or stoop in kindness to another as an superior to an inferior. Inferior is a person lower in rank, ability and status than another. Is that not my God and I? He's superior, I'm the inferior. He loves me just as I am. God will supply your needs as well as some of our wants. The Mercedes was a want not a need but a want.

> Or what man is there of you, whom if his son ask bread, will he give him a stone? (Matthew 7:9)

> If ye then, being evil, know how to give good gifts unto your children, how much more shall your Father which is in heaven give good things to them that ask Him? (Matthew 7:11)

Notes:

XIV

BREAKING THE ENSLAVING YOKE

When I was a young girl I thought christians were people who lived a perfect life. The way they would talk about the faults and mistakes of others. In my mind they did nothing sinful. Children were not allowed to take Communion because we didn't understand to take it you had to be sure you were approved by God. When the minister would ask if there were any reason you felt you couldn't take Communion to be excused. I made my exit. Even though I was saved I felt as if I weren't living the life He required of me. As I was leaving I would glance back at all the perfect people that remained and wonder how they did it.

Pray and ask God for wisdom, knowledge and revelation of His word. We all sin and fall short of what He would have us to be. We wake up in the morning to a brand new day, His mercies are new every morning. Start your day with a prayer of thanksgiving. Confess that you will rejoice and be glad in it. Strive to not allow anyone to ruin your day. Think that something good is going to happen to you and go forward with expectancy. When your mind tries to travel to what's bad, think of all thats good in your life.

Some people think God inflicts us with sickness and diseases to punish us for our sins. The wages of sin is death. I don't want this to be a woe is me testimony. I heard many testimonies from people that would make you sad instead of glorifying God for His goodness. Speaking things that are not as if they were activates our faith. It also causes God to move in our life.

My favorite bird is an eagle. Once I learned about his vision, strength and abilities to do certain things I was in awe about the creature he is. Made and designed by our Creator. If He gifted a bird with these abilities, can you imagine what He has given us? We are made in His image, a little lower than the angels. An eagle flies into a storm full speed, head up, and the impact from colliding with the storm allows him to rise above it. We don't have wings to fly but He gave us His word. His word can give us the strength to rise above and overcome every storm in our life. He gave us His word and the Holy Spirit as our Comforter. We need to use what He gave us before we turn to man for the things we are in need of. We seem to trust and believe man more than God.

Don't be sadden by trials. I want you to see how I was victorious and an overcomer by speaking the word of God. My blessings outweighed every trial I went through. With God nothing's impossible. We err but He doesn't love us any less. His love is undying and unfailing. The words we think and say effects us mentally, physically and spiritually. If you say I'm tired today, I don't feel like doing anything, you probably won't do anything. If you say I feel like I'm getting a headache, don't get it; let it stay wherever it is. Think other positive thoughts.

Say I forbid any sickness to operate in my body. It won't be easy, the more you try to do what's right the more Satan tries to persuade you to do what's wrong. Don't speak the word of the devil, speak the word of God. Speaking God's words destroys the devil's work. My faith and speaking God's word gives me victory to overcome the things of the world. God has given us His name (in the name of Jesus) and power against the things of the world. I won't allow myself or anyone to say I'm lucky. That I was lucky to overcome all that I've been through is an understatement, plus it lacks honoring God. Luck is a verb that means to succeed or prosper through chance, to come upon something desirable by chance. By chance means once in awhile, sometimes. I immediately correct them and say I'm not lucky, I was or am blessed. God's blessings are continuously upon me not by chance. Not once in awhile. I am blessed when I'm undeserving. His divine favor is forever upon us everyday, everywhere, at all times. I have a sign hanging in my house that says, "I'm not lucky, you don't know how much I've prayed." Couldn't resist buying that confirmation.

> Trust in him at all times; ye people, pour out
> your heart before him: God is a refuge for us.
> Selah. (Psalm 62:8)

Notes:

THE DEVIL THOUGHT
HE HAD ME

Some of the medical staff thought I was on my way out; to the point that I felt they wanted to give me my last rites. I said, "no, I'm good." They asked if I was sure, I replied "yes." They asked about my family. I told them I told my girls to go to work and to come after work. The next question was, would you like to donate any of your body parts? I said, "no, I need them all." It didn't register with me until later that they had counted me out. If I had known I would have told them not to count me out, God's got me. He's in control. Not today Satan, not today." He'd already spoken through someone else, "Satan you can't have her, she's mine; her heart belongs to me." So not today Satan or any day soon. I shall live and not die and declare the awesome amazing works of the Lord. I am doing this daily.

But I have raised you up for this purpose, that I might show you my power and that my name might be proclaimed in all the earth. (Exodus 9:16)

And being fully persuaded that what He had promised, He was able to perform. (Romans 4:21)

I prayed to the Lord and He answered me and freed me from all my fears. (Psalm 34:4)

And we know that in all things God works for the good of those who love Him, who have been called according to His purpose. (Romans 8:28)

Notes:

XVI

HE IS ...

I never asked why or felt the need to ask why these things occurred in my life. I knew there was a reason and asked whatever He wanted me to know and do to allow the Holy Spirit to reveal it to me. This I do know ; In my imperfection He was perfect. His Spirit was upon me and His word was within me being spoken out of my mouth. His word was my foundation and His word did exactly what He said it would do. Without faith it is impossible for these things to become reality.

Spend time, communication with God daily. Pray with expectancy. Try to be blessing to someone daily by a kind word or deed. Forgive and be willing to say "I'm sorry." Stop complaining and start proclaiming victory over your situation. Be the best you can be. Laugh, smile, let the inner you shine. Seek your purpose in your life. God didn't place us here just to be here. Do healthy things for your mind and body. Build your foundation of the word of God. You'll be able to stand when every thing seem to be falling apart. The best doesn't always happen but you can make the best out of what does happen. My mom used to say "I was bent, but never broken." I admired her strength throughout her life. I learned later in life that its okay to be broken. When you are broken you feel you no longer have the strength to fight your battles. When you are broken you are surrendering everything to God. It's when He can step in without your resistance and take complete control. He can mend that which is broken and restore all that's missing in your life. Let Him be what He wants to be to you. Remember He is everything we need. He is "I Am."

> And Moses said unto God, Behold, when I come unto the children of Israel, and shall say unto them, The God of your fathers hath sent me unto you; and they shall say to me, What is his name? what shall I say unto them? 14 And God said unto Moses, I AM THAT I AM: and he said, Thus shalt thou say unto the children of Israel, I AM hath sent me unto you. (Exodus 3:13, 14)

…: this is my name for ever, and this is my memorial unto all generations. HALLELUJAH